Praise for *Headstone*

"Gala upon gala" Mark Elber declares in his sumptuous, expansive volume of elegies, *Headstone*. Poignant, candid, fearless (and funny) odes and laments for the poet's father – and the poet's own life – come tumbling from this splendid book. Elber's tapestry of generations and culture begins in Eastern Europe, unfolds through the Holocaust, and finishes in New York and Israel, spanning births, marriages, and deaths. "An epigram wishing I were an epic . . . a narrative wading in a stream of consciousness," Elber draws us in with wordplay, long Ginsbergian lines, angst, and charm. The miraculous story of how his father saved his life – and how it ultimately saves the poet's own – makes this book a treasure.

MOLLY PEACOCK, AUTHOR OF *THE ANALYST: POEMS*

"Mark Elber is a poet who holds nothing back, a poet of profound connectiveness, who has the ambition to write 'These are love letters to the dead' and 'The future was yesterday' and the humility to balance that ambition with, 'Stop writing poetry and start waxing the car.' There will be no question about it. Here is the poem and here is the man. Throughout *Headstone* there are lines that insist I stop and read them aloud, and whole poems of heroic compassion and tenderness toward existence. With one book Mark Elber has given us both an elegy and a hosanna to what it is to be fully human."

RODNEY JONES, AUTHOR OF *VILLAGE PRODIGIES*

"Among these fragments reassembled from his life, from the recklessness of an American youth in Queens, from the struggle to understand parents who have endured the Holocaust, and later, in gratitude for a second marriage and for a son, Mark Elber makes poems shimmer with the incandescence of a lifetime."

BROOKS HAXTON, AUTHOR OF *MISTER TOEBONES*

"'What stitched together sounds can I offer?' Mark Elber asks in this moving collection. Eloquent through their gritty particulars, the poems of *Headstone* reclaim a Jewish past that, in Elber's hands, precipitates a resonant present. At their frequent and animated best, they convince with their textures, their rhythms, their emotional precision, and in their relentless, disarming attempt to account for what Coleridge called 'the whole ad hominem.'"

PETER COLE, AUTHOR OF *HYMNS & QUALMS:*
NEW AND SELECTED POEMS AND TRANSLATIONS

"Age-old questions – What are we from? Where are we going? In Elber's sometimes Whitmanic, sometimes Ginsbergian, always Elberian poems, in their alert detail and distances of time and place contained in spreading lines, in their mingling of catalogue and prayer, ode and anecdote, these questions feel urgent all over again. Elber makes the historic personal; the personal becomes myth and song. There's great mourning in this book – both collective and individual – but Elber also knows that 'the tongue will sing its sweetness' – maybe even in darkness."

DAISY FRIED, AUTHOR OF *THE YEAR THE CITY EMPTIED*

HEADSTONE

Copyright © 2022 Mark Elber
All rights reserved
Cover art: Margaret Singer
Cover design: Christine Drawl
First Edition 2022
Published in the United States of America
Printed by Spencer Printing
ISBN 978-1-7355148-5-7

Publisher's Cataloging-in-Publication
(Provided by Cassidy Cataloguing Services, Inc.)

Names: Elber, Mark, author.
Title: Headstone / Mark Elber.
Description: Baltimore, MD : Passager Books, [2022]
Identifiers: ISBN: 9781735514857
Subjects: LCSH: Elber, Mark--Poetry. | Jews--Poetry. | Holocaust, Jewish (1939-1945)--Poetry. | Emigration and immigration--Poetry. | Families--Poetry. | Heredity--Poetry. | LCGFT: Poetry.
Classification: LCC: PS3605.L293 H43 2022 | DDC: 811/.6--dc23

Passager Books
7401 Park Heights Avenue
Baltimore, Maryland 21208
www.passagerbooks.com

HEADSTONE
Mark Elber

Passager Books
Baltimore, MD
2022

עוֹלָם חֶסֶד יִבָּנֶה

The world is built by loving kindness

PSALMS 89:3

I said to myself: Redemption will come only when they are told, "Do you see that arch over there from the Roman period? It doesn't matter, but near it, a little to the left and then down a bit, there's a man who has just bought fruit and vegetables for his family."

FROM "TOURISTS" BY YEHUDA AMICHAI
TRANSLATED BY CHANA BLOCH

The artist must train not only his eye, but also his soul.

WASSILY KANDINSKY

To the memory of my parents
Gerson & Regina Elber

And to my beloved family
Shoshana, Lev & Mira

Contents

I
19. Requiem
20. Saturday
22. My Father's Hands
23. Further Notes From the Underground
25. I Am Therefore I Am
26. Ode to the Word
27. Red Hair
29. Prayers for the Dead

II
33. Headstone

III
49. Family Secrets
51. Blue
52. Résumé
54. February 5, 1922
55. The Belzer Rebbe Comes to Stryy
57. Pittsburgh
59. My Mother's Song
60. Ode to Accents
61. Personal Effects

IV
65. The Ingathering of Exiles

V
79. My Ex-Wedding
83. Blue Methuselah
86. "Such a Night"
87. Avishag the Shunamite
89. You and I
90. Moses Took a Second Wife
91. Beard
92. Your Small Hands
93. Red Walls
94. Praise
96. The God of Surprises

Requiem

My father went to sleep in his skin in the sun-flushed morning, in the flatlined morning
That shoveled a pit into my 35th year spadeful by spadeful and the sky collapsed over Queens

If I could, I'd revive the sound of his voice barely caught on a few bargain cassettes
The accent of his generation driven from the villages of their birth
The bellowing lung sacs of roosters squawking through the pebbled alleys, the straw beds, the well-stubbled streets of mud and stone

If I could replay the red hair of my youth, when Atlas stood five foot six in a stethoscope
Before we swallowed our love songs to each other
I'd exhume his spoken word lullabies, the chain of Slavic syllables that links me to his father's dark forests, to the kinks in his beard
To the warm lips buried in a riddled clearing
Ten thousand corpses deep

Saturday

I was born on a Saturday, 10:47 a.m.
An inch of snow coating Astoria, Queens
A mid-December day of sirens and corks jetting from dark chilled bottles
A day of bus exhaust belching blue-gray into the frigid air
Assembly lines greasing the cogs of America's wheels, stitching gloves for the coming frost
Trees in their barren beauty, the browns of bark climbing out of the planted sidewalks
Bountiful brick

The gardens of Sunnyside were mostly soil – dark, gritty, rocky and shrubbed, a dented hubcap or two, seeds in their deep sleep

In every borough there was singing in synagogues that morning, parchment unscrolled on felt-covered tables,
Chanting of Jacob's return to the wilderness of his youth, camels on the horizon bearing clay jugs
Smooth to the touch
Humps festooned with fig cakes, shawls draped on the soft hair of their backs

I was wrested out of the womb
Dumped wailing into the Western world, into a century wounded by wars

Lying on the belly of all that maternity
The web of veins, the life heaving in our chests, idling at a high pitch
In the 1951 of Hi-Fidelity, of housewives herded into suburbs
The Hit Parade of love and marriage, the promise of stainless steel

Tarnished from the vantage of my sparse coat of snowy hair, the brittle
    reward for those who wait
The whir of propellers in the distant background
The hum of the decades to come

My Father's Hands

held the blue globe, displaying the distance between our births
the slow trek of continents, the vast wet and dizzying spin
my mother singing to herself at the sink

his hands gripped the steering wheel
white walls and wide turns
the fat-assed fins of late 50's Detroit
the AM channel's chatter, songs squeezed between commercials
his foil-lined ashtray buried in the mentholated butts of Kools
subways rattling overhead

a collision of cultures between the front seat and back
the schoolyard banter native to New York
and an accent importing a world half an atlas away

refusing reparations for his snuffed-out generations
my father's hands split the unruly Atlantic
gently stroked my cheek

Further Notes from the Underground

I first rode the subway on my father's lap, on the broad seats of upholstered straw
The world was bigger then, streets steeper
I scrambled up the steps of the sky-high station, walked under the turnstile and made the long journey to the dinosaur bones in the universe of skyscrapers

I first rode the subway on my father's lap, on his gabardine coat in the clattering car, beside my humming mother, my New World brother, the ghosts of trolley cars sparking below
My small hands gripped his dark sleeve as we tunneled under the East River through the eardrum pressure, the car crammed with blank stares and cardboard ads for Luckies and Camels and slim women laughing against a backdrop of 80 proof

The years chugged by and the stars grew fainter in the Queens night
Hair cropped up in surprising places

I was half past twelve on the elevated platform when the Flushing local barreled into Bliss Street, jerked open its doors, and lured me away
From the oaths that echoed off the crushed stone underbelly of the El
From the nominal hedges and dog-drizzled hydrants
The parochial fists of my peers
The conductor's yawp leaving Sunnyside behind in a blur of dark brick and TV antennas blindly stabbing at the sky

I first met Walt Whitman in the robin's-egg blue cars suspended in view
    of my draft board
Between the winter Tet Offensive and the spring assassinations
Between the uniforms of Wall Street and the jeans of my generation
Oscar Williams made the introduction as I held the cold silver pole in
    my other hand
Above the huddled houses massed in view of the city's spires
Side streets stuffed with our fathers' wheels locked in "park"

The subway shuttled me to the World's Fair, to the gutted globe suspended
    in a fountain
A few years before Jimi's "Star Spangled Banner" fluttered in the
    shredding sky and regulation boots mired in the marshes of East Asia
I walked down the long ramps from Willets Point, the crowds congealing
    below
Staking my claim on the sinuous lines awaiting a glimpse of the future
    from GM, GE, and Ford – and all these years later I'm still waiting

From the dawn of my first stubble, from the taut reins in my parents'
    grip, from my muzzled declarations of independence, the IRT
    whisked me from the landscape of crumpled Budweisers, from the
    regnant polyester, from the crucified Lord of my neighbors glaring
    down at me every few blocks
So I stood on the local platform eyeing the expresses bolting by,
    emerging in the bearded Brooklyn of ecstatic prayer, the agnostic
    alleyways of the West Village

I Am Therefore I Am

I am the sea endlessly rinsing itself beside the ungroomed sand
I am the ubiquitous chain of ephemeral footprints
An epigram wishing I were an epic
A siren awaiting an Odysseus worthy of my allure
A surrealist temperament trapped in the body of a rationalist
Both "not-A" and "A" claiming the same logical piece of the planet

I am a narrative wading in a stream of consciousness
The phone rings
I am the silence on the other end of the line
I am undeclared income
I am off the books, off the record, off and running, off to a good start, off the deep end
I am the deep end
The steep ascent
Fear of heights
Height itself, absolute height

I am the blinding headlights which are nothing more than you racing towards your own reflection
I am the compulsory flaw
Pure melody afloat in rhythm
I am the child sacrificed on the altar of no god in particular

Ode to the Word

which knows no beginning
a cocoon of sound bursting into a radiant butterfly
grace incarnate

what rough squawk mutated into Scripture?
what gurgling infant harbored a psalmist?

tongue, magic carpet, luscious bed for a divine coupling
    of sound and sense
may you find an ear attuned to your music of doves in soft air,
    your crashing call wild with ocean

you took this nameless universe, dipped it in diphthongs
    and honey-smooth vowels enough to soothe an anxious yelp
a grunt, a guttural paradise, a heaven, was unsealed with a whisper
a heart heavy with longing and song, laid itself bare

may there be music enough a mouth might concoct with a string
    of sounds casting its spell
an alphabet conjuring the unimaginable

Red Hair

My father stirred the reddish dye in a plastic mug
    with a tongue depressor
painting his thin long strands that fell to one shoulder
stretching them ear to ear over the pale domed globe of his head

I'd enter the bathroom flushed with pushups and the strawberry
    flag of unruly curls
while he'd concoct his virile tint in boxers and sleeveless tees
to reverse the bleaching the years had wrought

in the house bordered by the stares of neighbors
hedges in the soil and soot
my father sought refuge in the tinge of his youth

used-car lots lined Queens Boulevard to our east
chains of plastic banners in the breeze above Detroit's fenders and fins
ten lanes of disrepair hauling to and from Manhattan

the green Q-60 bus lumbering back and forth
passing St. John's hospital where my father would later die
six floors above Queens Boulevard,

his name misspelled on his hospital door, on his death certificate

I've inherited his hands
the roots that loosed themselves but couldn't shake the black earth
　　of his birthplace
the low winter sun
the glare the years had softened
the flare of dusk

Prayers for the Dead

What stitched together sounds can I offer the silenced
blindsided by darkness
sealed with night under
a lid lathed from a tree and lowered
into the mute earth

what words that migrated out of the sea to slither
up the sibilant shore and offer a slew of grunts that slowly
found its own music
while the tongue groped
between stun and awe

here among the cries stoppered in their guttural glory
among pollen and seed, the trickle that births the torrent
before the senses grow senseless
and we are ebbing, humbled

our skin kissed each other awake
our voices break in the surge
as we resurrect the lush palette of touch
the divine dance radiant
the defiant song of generation

II

Headstone

I

Five stones perch on the family headstone
Five stones each the size of a child's fist
The Latin letters etched in the polished gray are large enough
    for the four of us
But no stone marks your parents' graves
No stones separate the thousands buried with them that day in a Polish
    meadow

On the family gravesite the grass is trimmed like your father's beard
Your father's beard that never had the chance to gray
On the family gravesite it is autumn and a squirrel stands on its hind legs
    devouring an acorn

A grandchild teethes in Boston
A grandchild closes the books your father lived by
He can no longer recall the alphabet which comes from another
    continent
Nor pronounce your father's name if he ever knew it
And there are no pictures in Boston of your parents
There are no pictures in Poland of your parents
There is no sign in the Polish forests of your father's labors there –
The trees that are gone are gone
Those that remain are fifty rings thicker

Flat stones skip through the placid waves on the Long
    Island harbor beach
Pebbles cushion the tanned feet summer after summer
As I am busy writing love letters to the dead
As I am busy watching the pebbles become sand
Letting the sand sift in ten thousand grains through my fingers

A hard rain pelts the harbor
Five stones are dislodged from the rough crown of the headstone in the
    Queens cemetery overlooking the site of the World's Fair where
    crowds gathered in 1939 with swirls of confection and the future
    was yesterday
1939 and the mass graves are almost ready
1939 and the sky is falling over Poland
It is autumn
It is autumn and you are walking through the chilling nights and the
    matted forests heading into the black sunrise, fleeing the Nazi west
    for the Soviet east
You are 31 and not yet my father
You have too many deaths to experience first
When you still were born in 1908
And hadn't yet patched over the last two numbers to erase certain years
When you stood in the white-robed clinics, short-haired and hopeful
And the war was no more than a threatening voice over the histrionic
    airwaves, but the west would protect us
And you hadn't yet met my mother
And your hands were so soft around a scalpel

You had a cousin in America who took your father's passage for this was
    a land of gangsters and your father wanted none of it

One generation passes down silence to the next
One generation seeks refuge in silence from the next
One generation suffers in silence from the next

II

I hear the air raid sirens, Jerusalem 1973
And in the shelter, I meet you worried that I flew back from France to
    land in a blacked-out metropolis and drive through the shuttered
    streets by the razor-thin headlights left when the blue paint dried
    over them
I meet you in Hadassah Hospital as I lean on the windowsill staring at the
    stubbled hills rolling out in every direction from the four paraplegics,
    smelling from thick stitched wounds, whom I turn every hour so
    their muscular bodies won't have bedsores and I still see the
    catheters and the smell stays with me for months
I hear you over my shoulder, turn, but only the accent remains
I see you in the shelter and by the windowsill, but your face resolves
    into another's
And I receive letters filled with instruction
How to be someone I'm not
How to wend my way out of the clouds into a wood-paneled office,
    diplomas above my head

How to stop being "pathologically religious"
How to look in the mirror and not recognize myself
Stop writing poetry and start waxing the car

III

I was born under the El in screaming distance of Bliss Street
I was born, Manhattan on the horizon, Galitzia at my back
Attended to by a microscope, a stethoscope, and a tongue depressor

You were born in the attic of your maternal grandparents' home where the borders migrate and the cold Carpathian Mountain air opened your lungs as you cried for the first time and it was February and it was a century just eight years old
I was born carrying your parents' names into the New World after the death of song, after the death of prayer, after the death of spring, and yet the sun still managed to break the buds out of the stillborn branches and stun each day with a limitless palette
And then you were six and your father went beardless into the First World War in an Austrian uniform as you moved to Vienna, a cousin's apartment, and it was school and German and two more brothers
(And I turned six with Walt Disney, toy soldiers, no grandparents, and the war always there with the chocolate milk, the hula-hoop, the tricycle, the baseball mitt and your English as a seventh language)

And you became a bar mitzvah, eldest male child of the eldest male
    child, your father away in the forest all week with his well-hewn
    face, with his growing piety, his foreman's position, measured
    words and muscular forearms
And your mother who cried before their wedding for the shearing of her
    hair which your father had spared as they sat in separate rooms a
    messenger running between till they met under a prayer shawl
    drinking the consecrated wine, stamping the glass into the oblivion
    it would share with the ancient Temple and so soon with all those
    drinking, dancing, and singing

And there were four children, three circumcisions, and two World Wars
And your mother fed you with counsel, warm breads, thick soups for the
    constant relatives, and the family looking to her as it would later
    look to you
After you saw the world by necessity
By trains to Nancy, France 1926
When the medical schools of Poland were locked to you as so many
    other doors would soon be, as the century matured, as the
    depression crushed Europe, as the world prepared to drown itself
    in fire
But you would survive by way of a Soviet uniform, as a Polish citizen
    discharged in Asia seeking a deeper Asia with the homeless,
    villageless, and country-less camped in a postwar Europe that
    had half swallowed them into its surfeited soil
You survived writing German from Asia to your brother David in Haifa
    believing your youngest brother, Bruno, alive though not knowing
    where

As Bruno did the same, believing you alive, not knowing where
The two cards meeting in Palestine written the same day, the same town –
And you wrote around the censors
You wrote around the black markets, the routine interrogations, under-staffed hospitals, overzealous informers, the shortage of everything but disease
You wrote of the birth of my brother Erwin – the true end of the war
But first one letter only Yiddish could convey – the death of your parents on *Hoshanah Rabbah* when the Nazis answered each prayer for salvation that shook your city from the cold iron of its barbed wired ghetto, from the exhausted hopes of its sleepless burial societies, from its fevered crannies of resistance, with the liquidation of the remaining survivors after they had unknowingly dug their own mass grave
And you carried that back to Europe where there were only scars to retrieve
And you carried that for three years in a DP camp healing others' wounds
And you brought it to Boston by boat two and a half years before my birth, Erwin on your lap, in your 41st June, over half your life over as you settled in New York in not quite one room on the Lower East Side

And you left Poland in the past and pieced together your own new world
With your first shingle in Sunnyside
And a robust used car followed by a new '55 green Mercury getting us from Skillman Avenue to Long Island on Sundays for your breaststroke

In the harbor in the bay in the ocean
And there was *JAMA, Reader's Digest,* and *Life*
And Robert Halls for our first baggy suits
And the socialist babysitter explaining canned laughter and pre-recording to any seven-year-old who would listen
And the troika of kosher butchers who supplied an aging Young Israel from their small sawdust shops, doubling as cantors with their piercing voices bringing melodies of a vanished Europe into the stout brick building of old chandeliers and shellacked wooden benches
Young Israel where I wanted to hush the congregants as you publicly mumbled blessings under your dark fedora
Where we sat near the rabbi looking at Mom in her women's section seat, donating a hundred for each of her raised fingers when appeal time came
Where I ran around the cement courtyard playing tag till my suit tore while you rose to cry for your parents four times a year

IV

Now I rise four times a year
And see you climbing an eighteen-foot ladder to the roof so I won't, six weeks before your death
I watch you in your white bathing cap swimming back and forth in the same Long Island harbor the last 30 years
Emerging firm and almost 80 in a blue cloth hat for your green folding

    chair, sunglasses, newspapers, and brown plastic sandals to walk
        home up the road
I see the squeezed tubes of reddish dye that take your hair back 40 years
I see your photograph, age four, shoulder-length locks and blond
The one family portrait, circa 1930, standing behind the fulcrum
    of your father
And you worked tirelessly in the office, in the hospital, in the house
    in your underwear in the basement hands always ending in tools
On the roof, in the yard, keeping your "he worships the car"
    spotless, tinfoil lining the unused ashtrays, the garage all but
    catalogued
The childhood eye charts I loved until I got old enough for us never to
    see eye to eye
From the time my forehead peeked above yours
From the time I stood on the elevated subway platform in the fall sun
    seeking high school somewhere on the Manhattan horizon, looking
    down on your office below
And I see us at the *Seder* table
Seated on your right, listening to the words you recite in an accent
    voicing the generations that end at this table where we hear the
    subway overhead, the huge planes descending on the blue-lit
    runways a few neighborhoods over, the local ocean that made
    all the difference
I see us at Young Israel, Yom Kippur eve, standing on the platform near
    the open ark, my arm around you once a year and I return to sleep
    in your concrete basement where I had studied so much contraband
    and family photographs

V

It is 1987
It is 5748
It is autumn
I awake 8 a.m. to put my suit back on for the full synagogue day
I hear running down the steps I recognize as mother reminding me of
>   the many panicked phone calls when you were hours late from the
>   hospital or Huntington or who knows where, but the electric
>   garage door finally opened and the tears retreated
You are sitting on your bed rocking and moaning, holding your chest
>   unable to dress
And the ambulance takes forever
I run into the street as it charges past the house wrong way down your
>   one-way street
A U-turn and up the narrow stairs bringing you down strapped
>   in a wheelchair for your heart is suddenly failing though you'd been
>   hiding nitro in your desk, in your glove compartment, in your
>   night table, for three years
And we are with you in the hurtling ambulance through the traffic lights,
>   on the curb, in the sunlight, no painkillers
And they're asking me questions as you're moaning against your will –
>   your name, address, age
And I accurately say 79 which you amend through the spasms to 77
I see you giving me the food off your plate if I was still hungry
And they keep you for hours in the emergency room because you
>   won't stabilize

They keep me out till I'm summoned at last, and your first three words
    are "Don't tell Erwin"
Then you're in the coronary care unit
And I'm on the phones – to Erwin, to your brother, Bruno, to a heart
    specialist
And you're there for 12 days
Tubes in your nose, long hair hanging off the side of your head, constant
    monitoring
You start to improve and Bruno, still planning to visit Israel, comes to
    the hospital, sits by your right bedside, I sit by the other
You ask will he take you
"Are you ready?"
"I am, but my body isn't"

Bruno speaks of not going, glances at me and bursts into tears, Bruno
    whom I've never seen cry, burying his face in your blankets and
    we shake, sobbing with him
He leaves – your condition worsens severely
I see myself August 1960 in the airport in Israel as you come to join us
    after five weeks apart – I'm wearing sunglasses to hide my tears
Erwin flies in again with a suitcase and a dark suit
It's all day in the waiting room taking turns by your side
And you brush your teeth vigorously, sit up in bed briskly, and I shave
    you for the first and last time – the soft foam against your full cheeks

I remember sitting in the back seat so many thousands of miles
How you sped into the driveway, the housecleaner asking if you ever
    raced cars

And you asked for a prayer book – tomorrow was *Hoshanah Rabbah* –
    so you could say *Kaddish* for your parents, telling me your father's
    words have nourished you to this day
And I see you in your paneled office offering advice
I see you visiting me in your hospital when my tonsils are removed,
    driving 400 miles to bring Erwin there as his appendix bursts
    on the operating table
I see you at my wedding dancing one hand in the air, though I knew
    you didn't approve
Leaning your head against your sister's bedroom wall in Haifa crying
    when confusing the bug bites on my forearm with needle tracks
I see us arguing for hours after Erwin's son Niles' bar mitzvah till your
    anger bursts as you cry you're "not a perfect father"
I hear you ask where the five points missing from a hundred on my
    ninth-grade report card are
I see the faces of the unfamiliar children you found to play with me
    in the park when you didn't want to
I see you hold the back of my bicycle as you teach me to ride,
    running beside me

And you are in your office weighing, measuring, giving pills, injections,
    kisses
You are waxing the car
You are in your white examining robe
You are in your gray suit called to the Torah
You are with your siblings in Israel, all in your seventies, all dressed
    in blue

You are driving Erwin to medical school in Boston unloading the car
	into his basement apartment, so upset he'll get no daylight that
	we drive straight back
I see you at Erwin's med school graduation, at my college commencement,
	at Niles' circumcision
And now I hear you say *Kaddish* in the coronary care unit, your voice
	breaking on the last day of your life

VI

In the cemetery, in our torn lapels, unshaven, your coffin lies beneath
	the family headstone in the open ground
Erwin takes the shovel and drops earth and stone onto the smooth
	wooden Jewish star lying below in the sunburst October on the
	hill overlooking the unisphere, airplanes roaring out of La Guardia
And I take the shovel to move more of the mound of raw earth
I hear the stones hit the wood
I feel the stones hit the wood
I see your wooden Long Island home tended so carefully
I see your hands on the wooden kitchen table, your soft cheeks, thin
	nose, slim legs, slight stomach, cloth blue slippers, light blue eyes,
	stethoscope round your neck
I hear the roll of your r's
I see us walking home together from the synagogue on your last night
	outside a hospital and see myself kissing you goodbye though you
	were no longer there

And if I ever have children, they will never know my father as I never
 knew yours
And Niles takes the shovel and adds earth
And adds earth
And adds earth.

III

Family Secrets

When the dawn bombs blitzed Poland
Gutting buildings, blasting the past off course

My parents, destined to never cross paths,
Sixty-two miles and a deity apart
Suddenly veered towards each other

When black moustaches severed Poland between them and the white lab
    coats of the Reich were steeped in poison gas
When paranoia was proof of sanity, my father stored a stiletto in his
    calf-length boots
Walking the night forests of forged identities and stolen lugers
    from Cracow to the Russian East

Before the ghettos were wrapped in barbed wire
And the crooked cross plunged its crippling stake wherever it could
He kept walking under moonlight, surviving on roots

Watching other Jews herded in a town square
He weighed the risks of capture and compliance
And continued

With Berlin breathing down his neck, he reached his home finding
    himself drafted into a Soviet uniform
Kissing his parents goodbye

Scraping the whiskers from his face
Leaving his copper hair open to the sky
Leaving the terrified attics and their tremble

To ride the military trains, suture the skulls of soldiers at Stalingrad
Where the woman who would hemorrhage me into the New World
And name me in memory of his parents
Handed him his scalpels

Blue

My first blue was the blanket huddling my body's heat
a cocoon of twilight and cotton
cushioning the coarse fall into the world of men

Blue bubbled up between the cracks in the black and white world
seams that started to fray, sounds that crackled on stations the needle
    never quite nailed
a tone hovering between a stifled cry and a gasp in the hush
and what music of amplified strings and skins still clutching the catch
    in the throat
in their taut stretch
in their hum and vibration
in their sting released, unleashed, in the resin, in the unpolished
    and undertones
in the honey trickle

Blue was a red beard whitening on a face rushing flush into the future

And where will all this lead?
from the first taste of blueberries in a white bowl rinsed with
    a hand pump,
poured from a cardboard pint carton
juiced in the mouth and the tongue will sing its sweetness

Résumé

Somehow I was born, though my parents could never explain it –
Either I stepped off a train from Cracow or a conveyor belt in a milk
    processing plant in urban Queens –
Cried, eructed, and was generally happy.
I was weaned on borscht
Did not discover the chickpea till way past puberty

I started school with the mandatory tears
In those years the world was still flat
Till a fourth-grade class trip threw me off balance racing round the
    Rawson street subway stop landing me in a field of breasts –
And so began my higher education

I wandered from the echo under the El to the Hayden Planetarium to
    weigh myself on the moon or Venus or anywhere but Queens
I closed my bedroom door in search of natural history
Discovering my arms were long enough

And I began to read –
Road maps, exit signs, Masters & Johnson
I began to love the smoldering kiss of the horizon
Love the silence of the dark a.m. hours
Love myself to sleep

And when I wake facing an ancient tomorrow
When my head is a compass that can find no north
And I try to retrace my wandering steps these last 40 years in search of a
    wilderness
From when I first walked the earth belly to belly
From when I first craned to stare back at the stars and mistook God
    for warm milk or the voice behind rough hands
Knowing it is not good that man should be alone
That he should compose love songs only for his own two ears
Leave the bark uninscribed
Have no smile or scent or oasis of jewelry to dislocate his sleep
It is not good to coax the apple out of the tree and not know the blessing
    of another's mouth
Having the heart beat only against itself

February 5, 1922

On my father's 14th birthday, the ink was drying on Rilke's notebook
The Sonnets to Orpheus having found the fingers to release them

Nine years before Dali's clocks began to droop, weep, drape the landscape
The German mark was being unmoored and all Europe would pay

When heads of axes were being buried in the thick bark of trees
Forearms bulging in the grip of angry muscle
My father's inflammatory hair, his polyglot silence
Were simmering in the eastern ends of Poland

Before broths began to thin
Tubers dominate dinner
And the beer halls turn rowdy
In the year of the birth of the Soviets
In the year Ulysses spoke English in Paris with a brogue

The Belzer Rebbe Comes to Stryy

And no one knew the War would come
That the dancers' beards would be torn from their faces in the same
 public squares where they'd danced with their white shirts leaping
 out of their pants, with their black hats falling over their eyes,
 with their feet forgetting every ache in the wonder of being alive
Fear was familiar like staying home locked and shuttered on Christmas
But this day the streets belonged to the throngs greeting the Belzer
 Rebbe in his wide-brimmed hat and long black coat, his pockets
 full of pleas – shoes for the children, wool for a sweater, oil for
 the lamp to read by at night
And the children came on their fathers' shoulders where Heaven is
 within reach
And fathers danced with those small bodies aloft like sacred scrolls
 under the cirrus sky
Everywhere the Rebbe turned he saw flowers twisting towards the sun
 though the earth is dusty and well-trodden, though weeds spread
 unwatered
The Rebbe saw all that made the feet heavy of the dancers encircling
 him and this made his feet heavy too
He heard the sobs swallowed up in the joyous melodies of the high-
 pitched voices and he gulped deeply
His stomach growled with their hunger, his mouth parched, his eyes
 welled up

And he danced with abandon in the closed-off square
>   for they needed him to
And he sang through the breaks in his voice
And though God is so well hidden in the acts of the stranger, in the
>   drunken gangs of cross-town Saturday nights, in the hunger
>   heard in the beggar's cry, in the mortal fevers of children
The Rebbe must dance to hasten the day when every street will draw
>   a song from our feet, when everyone will be their own Rebbe
And the thousands of footprints made one vast mosaic effaced in the
>   wide-broomed morning
And years later that day was transported in slivers to other Polish villages –
Sobibor, Treblinka, Auschwitz
Nine-tenths of the memory vanished there,
But the Rebbe was smuggled beardless to Palestine over his protests
For his wish was to share his followers' fate, the one thing they
>   couldn't suffer
And the Rebbe's beard slowly grew back under the blue skies and narrow
>   alleys of Jerusalem
But his feet, his feet, never danced again.

Pittsburgh
for my only brother

My brother never set foot in the Pittsburgh of his birth
The Pittsburgh of overwrought rivers and chain-smoking stacks
Chuffing illegible signals in the pig iron dawn

It was a bloodless birth in a traumatized decade
A household of fictional memories
An impossible future
Half Looney Toons, half Zyklon B

My brother never beheld the Vienna of his birth where the sweet string sections went badly out of tune a decade earlier
Though his first words emerged in German under his blond head
Though he picked wild berries in the Austrian hills for our father
Shy, delicate, blue
Before I was even an afterthought, a bookmark in a travelogue stalled in the borough of Queens

Approaching America
My brother sat on our mother's lap inhaling the fine spray as the brine clapped against the steep cold sides of the ship slipping into Boston Bay
The summer solstice only weeks away
The assault of English on his four-year-old ears

But first the Hebrew Immigrant Aid Society housed them in a room on
    Manhattan's Lower East Side
Soot caking the burgundy bricks
The stew of accents
The relief of hydrants, black and fluted, in the humid summer streets
The incessant hacking of the boy next door

I can't blame Pittsburgh for our nervous coughs
Our mother's contagious fears
Our father's unremitting expectations
Our failed first marriages

My brother could not outrun the burden of the first born in whom
    all hope is placed
As our mother recalled each lost brother and parent

And even though she would never see the landscape that mined and
    smelted ore
Steeling the west, pulverizing rock
Pittsburgh was a safe place to be born
Even after the fact.

My Mother's Song

My mother sang to console herself, to keep the years of bare cupboards
    at bay
Shield herself from memories of typhus and typhoid, from the sweats
    and shivers of soldiers she nursed into the next world
She sang to the young woman she once was – bereaved, bewildered,
    bombarded on a train from Stalingrad

Her voice carried cries that straddled an ocean, prayers stomped at the
    pit of the throat that even a deaf god might hear

My mother sang at the sink, remembering tastes long turned to ash with
    pre-war Poland
The sting of horseradish smothering the sweet fish, the cabbage leaves
    coddling the spiced ground beef, rice, and raisins
The oral lore kneaded into braided breads
The drizzle of honey

Her voice muffled the shrieks of children who didn't outlive November
    1941, buried under the bulk of their parents

My mother would one day laugh again with abandon but for the broken
    glass always in the background
Hum in loud dresses gathering friends in the dining room under the
    chandelier
Singing the multi-tongued melodies of the exiled

Ode to Accents

When I open my mouth people hear Second Avenue Deli, pastrami
    on rye, sour pickles, rattling tracks of the local to Shea Stadium,
Queens Boulevard staring at Manhattan's skyline

I affect the sound of falafel, bourekas, babaghanoush, but everyone
    hears latkes sizzling in the background

When my parents opened their mouths people heard borsht, stuffed
    cabbage, gefilte fish, Slavic winters
Each "w" a "v," each "th" a "t"

They never spoke to me in their mother tongues
Preferring the language of my native New York, hoping I'd blend in,
    like they couldn't

Our names bore our ancestors on our backs from one exile to another
A covenant of sound stretching back to the craggy hills of Jerusalem,
    the caves of Qumran
A shibboleth awaiting its resurrection

The words of my parents
A living link to the world turned to ash by 1945

Personal Effects

Blues band jamming up the street

harmonica cupped in a gold-ringed hand
keening in the ear of a mic
heaving its heart into the cold metal and its sheen

the snarl of guitars, a voice full of gravel and scars

Eighth Avenue outside the maraschino red door
deaf to the vocals riveting the room
with its smoke, cramp, and amps strewing sound
from the hum and core of their simmering tubes

a solo's notes kin to the dark resin lodged in the tables' knots
callused fingertips scaling a '62 Fender's frets
coaxing its secrets through a slur of vibrato moans

tremolo and bellow, undertow of sound,
part piano, part snare and kick,
licks that lift, lift, and lift

IV

The Ingathering of Exiles
(at 33 Rechov Ramban, Jerusalem)

I'm finally in love and we must part
America has invaded Cambodia
It's midnight as I descend the long steps from the campus library to meet
    a mounting demonstration
The delicate stench of New Jersey refineries wafting into West Philadelphia
And rock 'n' roll without the music
And Ira with a megaphone irate and I am too

I am in love and Fellini's *Satyricon* is sweeping the screen as we kiss
    for the first time before the revolution
And I will try to convince the Sunday Men's Clubs while their mouths
    are full of lox and orange juice that aggression is sending the planet
    down the river, that you cannot un-burn the napalmed civilian,
    that human skin has too short a shelf-life as it is
I am reading *Do It* according to the author's instructions
Led Zeppelin's debut saturates my room as I steep in the dark a.m.
    stupor of sleeplessness
And I volunteer in the neighboring ghetto renovating a flooded
    basement and raking a wheelbarrow full of sand, water, and
    limestone to seal the visible damage
But I have no guilt, for Hitler failed to stop me from singing
    "All You Need Is Love," but forced me to sing in English
And the summer is a fortuitous mixture of heat and heat

   · *33 Rechov Ramban: 33 Ramban Street*

As we walk by the Delaware River out of which Philadelphia crawled, spawning sidewalks and universities

We break a watermelon against a bleached curb and you ask: "Are you going to do me tonight?"
To which I respond with the flight of the bumblebee pollinating lush lotus gardens and that I could only make love with you, when I meant to say "God willing"
And we lay on the thin mattress on the ground floor in your parents' house where we hear the robin's lullaby
And I always feel the need to say "forever"
Though I am a loner with a few notebooks and a collection of ballpoints
We are dawn's offspring flushed with color, cloth belts and turquoise love beads
Thriving on crowds, amplified music and drawn-out sunsets seen from the highest available altitude

And I am in love, but taking El Al flight double-oh something, overpacking my bags
And only my mother knows how to cry in public
It will take my father three more airports and two more years
And this is a dress rehearsal for many long goodbyes
This is a group flight and a group photograph of strangers thrown together in a mock-up of who's who on the one-year overseas program and one day they will all return to being the nameless faces they started as
And my father fails to convince me to leave *Revolution for the Hell of It*

behind, so I read it five miles above the Atlantic under the small overhead beam illuminating Abbie Hoffman in the otherwise sleeping cabin

In the mid-flight morning I discover your first confession of love in a folded note stowed away in my *Tefillin* bag

Across the aisle I spy a co-conspirator underlining his way through Jerry Rubin

We will become roommates after we collect our luggage, after we summon our fatigue in slept-in jeans, after we are whisked down to the desert to meet the Milky Way a few hours before it retires for the morning

We stock up on sweet wafers and aerogrammes commiserating about this endless exile of the heart, how our emotional endurance is being pushed past its limits

The parched earth is cracked all around us, we cannot quench our thirsts, we cannot talk our way out of our longing, and we cannot believe it's been only one day

But I will spend my afternoons sweating under the sun, reading bareback on a bunker, knowing nothing of the lives that squeezed under this hot concrete block

And I am an American in the Negev as the tour guide pointed out to his busload of air-conditioned tourists barging through the middle of *The Electric Kool-Aid Acid Test*

I am a conscientious objector for God is one and the desert one and the white stone and palm-treed oasis at the end of the canyon below us, one

The ibexes refreshing themselves in the dusk pools of algae and moist minerals, one

And you, my love, seven time zones away planning to backpack through Europe and run into me on a Saturday night street in residential Jerusalem after not writing me for three weeks, one

And the divided citizenry, one

The echoless burnt hills and huge craters and overpopulated housing developments, one

The nomads with their camels and jeeps and oral histories, one

The peoples staring at each other across border telescopes, plotting and replotting, threatening, mourning, blessing, burying and decomposing under the feet of anthem singers and demagogues, one

The loose collections of words, glances, unbarterable exchanges, the million meanings of touch, the grand cacophony of birds, surf, and silence, one also

And the world is standing still at the speed of light

I am tripping down the snake path at Masada seeing every step as the major event it is

Phantom jets flying in formation above the excavated mosaics and ritual bath

You can see the work of nameless hands 2000 years ago shaping the diminutive tiles as they slowly color my image of who I have been

And I do not plan to give the world insurance policies

I do not plan to give teeth fillings

I do not plan to devise tax shelters for the landed gentry

I do not plan to live with four flat mates in a rarely locked apartment
    among the older cypress and pine trees of Jerusalem, but do
And now I should tell you about Cheryl, but she deserves her own poem
Now I should tell you what happens to this boy from Queens in the
    middle of Jerusalem, in the middle of a college education, in the
    middle of the 60's though it's 1970, in the middle of discovering
    one is always in the middle till the very end

Five lives converged on 33 Rechov Ramban across a wheel-shaped table,
    six brands of cigarettes, sugar sweetening many a black instant
    coffee, a small GE stereo built for the voyage from Essex Street
    with its sour pickles and nostalgia
And I am recounting this under the gothic spell of my father's red
    manual typewriter and the interlacing streets I will never see the
    same way again
I am recounting this to the tune of "Hatikvah" and Hendrix's "Star
    Spangled Banner" and remind me to make room for "The Dream
    Is Over"
I am writing this under the glare of army searchlights scanning the hills
    as we walked to Bethlehem X-Mas eve, Nasser has died and Black
    September has erupted to our east, Sephardic Black Panthers are
    jailed for being Sephardic Black Panthers and we have only begun
    to march, but right now we are pilgrims from the very earthly
    Jerusalem and that is cause for celebration
And I have squeezed my share of prayers between its inscrutable stones,
    and they say God with the big ears is listening, they say we of the
    last great sunsets have forgotten that in the beginning was awe

· *Hatikvah: The Israeli National Anthem (literally: "the hope")*

And I am always longing for the next great beginning
I am laughing in the living room in once white tennis sneakers and
    my brother's fading tan corduroy sports jacket with the pockets
    built around paperbacks
We are playing chess as a form of foreplay
And you gently take my king and take my king

And this is in honor of the five weeks to the day we spent half our lives
    in a bedroom
I wake up to the soft miracle of your mouth
Or you wake up to my tongue too busy to talk
And I celebrate turning 19 in bed

And this is in honor of the hills born around Jerusalem and the carob
    fruit bearing Old World beads of honey in its brown-thick pods
This is in honor of the sun teaching one to leave quietly but with a big
    impression
And I am still learning to listen – to the fluorescent lamp above the desk
    where I write, the phosphorous flaring at the tip of the wooden
    match, the hum of the escalator taking you up to Boarding and
    America
And I am just learning to look – at the curtained libraries behind
    flowerpots of domesticated cactus, at the streets that stare straight
    at the sun, at the eyebrows of the midtown mime as he lifts his hat
    off his bald head hoping for loud money, at your teeth barely
    imprinting your lower lip at the cusp of a shudder

And I was never on my way to India though I made it to the Western
  Wall, the Jerusalem Forest, the open market of still shivering chickens
  and lead weights telling you how much grapefruit, persimmons,
  cracked olives, or kohlrabi is weighing down your blue plastic
  baskets and will cover your kitchen table for five dollars
We were at the crossroads between worlds, on the trade routes of Africa,
  Asia, and Europe, somewhere between the grandparents I never
  knew and the grandchildren I may never know, somewhere between
  a torch-light procession up a night-soaked Masada chanting
  "Let My People Go" and the Joshua light show pulsing to "I'm Free,"
  somewhere between *The Ten Commandments* and *2001*
We were brought together by student loans, Jewish summer camps and
  scarred parents
We were brought together because on our way back from the Wall
  a beggar stopped me putting my hand on his herniated stomach
  making the sale
We were brought together by long hair, liberal arts, and 200 people
  needing a place to crash in Jerusalem
We were brought together because we spoke the common language
  of denim, hookahs, and sleeping bags on beaches, stairwells, and
  parking lots that today are five-star hotels and nothing's as innocent
  as it seems

We were brought together because the long-haired septuagenarian
  sculptor and his medical hypnotist wife needed neighbors and
  Danny, Kenny, Mark, Rick, and Sol needed a home and Jerusalem
  needed some exiles from Woodstock Nation

Someone had to keep the party going
Someone had to disseminate Beat literature to the bearded and to the braless
Someone had to usher in the Sabbath in a suit and sneakers
Someone had to break the news that television is one long commercial

And you know, I should have never lent my hand-made love beads to the sixteen-year-old Orthodox girl who promised to return them at the starlit fork in the road the next night and left me only the starlit fork in the road which was a greater gift I still don't totally fathom
And I was poised between the West with its roads full of horsepower and horizons and the Middle East which could have housed the haven I never had
I was poised before seven years of growth and seven years of growing confusion, seven years of affection in abundance and abundant disaffection – and they were all the same seven years
And I don't know how much to reveal
For I was just learning to love and to struggle for independence for the next 20 years
And I was not surprised that my parents read my mail
I was not surprised that my desk drawers were fair game

But I *was* surprised to get an unsigned typewritten six-page letter from my father the August day after coming down the snake path to float in the Dead Sea sitting cross-legged in the buoyant waters with a circle of friends, the deep blue of the sky washing out, ringed by the desert mountains, hiking to the falls of Ein Gedi where the waters wash through the green cracks in the sunbaked surroundings,

  where the waters trickle past huge boulders, where the waters fall
  from one peak to another and I watched them fall over my
  face, all over my face
And the next noon I crashed into my father's letter
I crashed into six pages of open wounds
I crashed into my whole life paraded before me and you know what?
I didn't recognize it
But I also didn't recognize my father's pain
I didn't recognize you could spend nineteen years running from one
  womb to another – and there's a holy grail if ever there was one
And I didn't recognize *my* pain either, turning it into dramatic readings
  of something so raw it left us in stitches
And I never quite grasped the domino theory directly linking masturbation
  to the New Left
And how all of this explained my only getting a B in calculus
But those letters were surely impatient to be read, languishing in my
  drawer, as my father, stirred by some paternal moral imperative,
  pried my dresser for evidence of my allegiance to "the best minds
  of my generation" – and hit pay dirt
And I couldn't see past the upper-case threats and underlined ultimatums,
But I tried to believe I didn't care
I tried to exorcise my economic dependence by every which way
  but work
And I needed the space of an ocean or two to feel free from the head
  to foot scrutiny of 40 years of clinical experience
So began a correspondence culminating face to face as the rainy season
  threatened and Jerusalem started sleeping with its windows shut

I found myself at 1 p.m., three blocks from 33 Rechov Ramban, my
    father insisting on stopping in as two bearded crashers slept in
    my room – the future Shabbtai and Chaim who that day were
    still very much Stuie and Harvey – my father swooped by and
    stormed out yelling I can't have such friends
"You can't tell me who my friends can be"
Stuie later adding: "good thing he couldn't see my dreams"
And we board a bus to go anywhere reaching the Hebrew U. station
    where bags are frisked for bombs and my father fumes I "can't have
    such friends"
He is shaking
He is seeing Harvey's head buried in the pillow, his hair spilling on the sheets
He is seeing his son tie his own shoelaces, not follow in his footsteps
He is seeing books the Soviets would have banned demonstrating around
    the house
He is shaking, saying he will kill me, he will kill me, himself and my
    mother too who replies: "not me!"
And I'm thinking I should run, hide till they leave, take a job, anything
I should go to the bathroom in the first building I find, outside which
    my mother advises don't aggravate him, agree to anything, then do
    what you want
She is the amnesiac witness, she is a fount of family myth, she is a singer
    at frequent parties with a loud laugh and louder dresses
My father waits on a low stone bench with two photographs –
    one of Timothy Leary sitting on his knees, the other my brother
    in comparable posture holding his year-old son convincing my
    father that my brother too is a psychedelic experimenter
He begins to cry: "Where did I go wrong?"

And I offer him anything
For he is the Wailing Wall where he wanted me to swear to my conversion
    to his principles of faith
I believe in perfect faith that I should cut my hair and shave my
    "silly beard," obey my parents and not immature professors
For surely I am the will-less pawn hiding among the liberal arts
I am the damaged DNA disgracing the martyred ancestors
I am the son who eats too little meat
I am the son who takes God too seriously
I am the son who finally succumbed to wearing a hairnet to sleep at the
    age of fourteen before all control was lost
I am the son who confused Kaddish with a great poem
I am the son who perceived his father out of proportion
I am the skewed proportions
I am the lost control
I am the endless adolescence with overdue books
I am the diminishing hope of survivors
I am my grandfather's chin under a scraggly red beard
I am the living memory of the errors of my uncle's ways, of his
    grandfather's straw-filled barn in the Polish countryside as police
    combed for communist agitators
I am the agitation, the blue-eyed agitation
I am the contraband snuck through the border whispering "Russia, Russia"
I am the six-word profession of faith, one for each million who died in vain
I am the lost address-book with the smudged print
I am my father's burnt library
I am my father's letters

I am too much my father's son
I am the lost childhood wandering in the cordoned-off streets of
 Jerusalem, Independence Day, with the plastic hammers singing
 on skulls, with the fragrance of fried fat filling sidewalks, with the
 crowds coming from a hundred different directions, from a hundred
 different countries for a hundred different reasons watching the
 sky fill with fireworks from the Chief Rabbinate's roof and the
 night is streaked with color and your ears are flushed with a dozen
 languages and your mouth fills with a dozen tastes and a dozen
 non sequiturs and a dozen incipient kisses and why doesn't this last
 forever instead of ending one day back in the hilly heat of summer
 labeling boxes that send my life back into exile till the coming
 generations.

V

My Ex-Wedding

At my ex-in-laws
A sunny late August surrounds the expectant canopy, a black and white
    prayer shawl on four underfed poles
With the thick-necked Throgs Neck Bridge in the backdrop
And a broad Bronx horizon

After fasting from each other for a week
I enter the woman-filled bride's room and lower your sheer veil
The males singing me back out
Beards in abundance
With the rabbis bringing two genuine Brooklyn God-fearing witnesses
    to the ceremony half filled with Holocaust survivors who left their
    faith in Europe

And I am groomed in a white robe in a red beard in gold-rimmed
    glasses and a black sash dividing my upper half from my lower half
And my upper half remembers the days
While my lower half remembers the nights
And my lower half thinks it's my upper half
But my upper half thinks
And the days began one night when you smiled at me from our freshman
    directory under the glare of my tensor lamp
And I don't believe in fate
You barely believe in marriage
Our parents are in disbelief

And our friends are hungry
I am under the canopy as you approach and circle me seven times
I am under 22 and under the impression I'm an adult
And every rabbi calls me a "king" in the eyes of the tradition and then
    summons me like a page to his office
But I am well-trained in adolescence
And I am afraid of my father and can't admit it
I am afraid of tomorrow and don't know it
I feel no fear
I am beaming, for Juliet is the sun
And the wine is waiting in the rabbi's palm
The pale gold ring is waiting in my brother's pocket
The ancient Temple is waiting to be remembered
And on the heels of the muffled shatter of glass wrapped in a cloth napkin
    the band erupts and the food breaks out and we forget how we've
    been legislated around every corner –
Our love is now legal in New York
The children we will one day never have would be legitimate
And even God approves

Is this what you meant sitting on the edge of the stone pool saying you
    wanted to marry
As we were growing up together
As we were discovering ourselves
As we were discovering ourselves in each other
Spending months on the way talking till dawn
Thrilling to the light touch of our fingertips passing a lit cigarette
    because our lips had not yet been introduced

Is this what we meant?
Did our bodies mean to become strangers so quickly after slowly becoming fast friends?

I was barely 19 when we met, you were almost 21
We were a festival waiting to be founded
We were flesh closing over an open wound
And you brought your suspicions, I brought my guilt
And so our parents met
Our fathers talking turkey
Our mothers speaking mink
And what could we think
Having already played house for two years
And our pre-marriage counselor telegraphs congratulations from Toronto
And our parents telegraph criticisms from all over the place

And we were warned not to marry while the moon was waning
We were warned not to stare at the late August sun from under a makeshift canopy
And how did we get there?
Through the jealousies
Through the letters burning in tin trash baskets
Through all the threats to never live happily ever after at the top of our lungs
How did we get there?
On the way to embracing across a white handkerchief, two lone chairs dancing in the air

Would we ever be this close again?
And under the yellow canvas tent in the backyard whirling in separate circles till we burst out of orbit, hands fondling the air, throats throwing biblical mating calls across the trampled lawn and my brother breaks in out of nowhere in 20 years to twirl with me around the close circumference of blood on blood
And I want to cry on his collar and laugh two pent-up decades worth
But sing instead
Words only our feet understand
And the ground feels like it will hold us up forever as four friends held up the fragile poles supporting the prayer shawl under everyman's sky and everywoman's sky and every sky that ever lived –
But nothing stands still long enough
Not the sun on August 26th
Not the immortal feelings of nineteen
Not the smile that rivets you to a stranger's face in a book of student photographs
Not the first kiss that promises to place a whole world naked before you and delivers
Not the last glance across the white bridge of a handkerchief when your entire weight is suspended in air and you find privacy in each other's eyes while the world below is staring at you
Not the frail canopy that folds like a stretcher and takes its magic show around the next blind curve.

Blue Methuselah

The odometer turned over in the middle of my 28th year
Two tents in the trunk, top 40 on the radio, three lives meeting in my
    hand-me-down Valiant
Thanks to the Ride Boards of Lower Manhattan
The pull of the flailing Pacific, the cobblestoned streets hobbling to the river

The chassis showing its age, the radiator barely holding in its hiss
The twilight blue cushions of faux leather hoarding their loose change
We leave the simmer of August NYC for the metallic gait of the G.W.B.
Spanning the shimmering Hudson

Plowing through the Midwest
Towards the loud Wisconsin rain on the taut plastic fly hammered
    down in the dark
The chaff and grain, the colonies of corn
The hormone-heavy cows and their rough udders
The manured past still evident in the breeze

The odometer turned over on a Montana mountain pass
Water rappelling down the precipice, wind fluttering the wild pink petals
Tomorrow pressing against the windshield at 80 miles an hour

Methuselah's six cylinders carried us north where Canada greeted us
    with suspicion
Ruffling toiletries, underwear, the ash left lining the tucked-in tray

And we pitched our tents on the Kampgrounds of America
On the soil not yet mauled by brand names
Not yet squeezed under a narrowing sky

And what drove this foot to flatten on the floorboard
Drove the cranes that raised cities out of the foddered heartland
The sledgehammers slamming stakes into the bullied earth

Methuselah hums at 2000 rpm
I crank down the window to better hear the asphalt whooshing under the white-walls
Rest my elbow on the door ledge, thump a rhythm on the sun-blanched roof
Despite the open road long past its expiration date
The vast interstate system of dead ends

And once upon a time there was August 1980
There were three strangers crossing a continent
With their 20-odd years apiece
With their backpacks, hiking boots, and one broken marriage
With their blues, their blue jeans, their blue and brown eyes and cheap cameras blinking at the long plains from the Poconos to the Badlands

A guitar camped in the back seat jangling melodies
To the granite-jawed Presidents peering from Dakota peaks
To 18-wheelers carting vegetables across the country

To the CB gibberish, to the hooves racing across the highlands,
    vultures hovering over stretches of highway
Steel teeth chiseling through the gristle of mountains

Your loose blouses begging me to look though I needed no coaxing
Waking beside meadows once trampled by cannon and cavalry, cries of
    blood muffled in furrowed turf
Watching freight trains snake along riverbeds and prairies, dark cattle
    cars clacking to the pulse of driven steer
Wyoming's geysers burst against a clear sky, unstoppered spray
Dancing in a dark pub in Northwest Washington, "Beast of Burden's"
    last bars prying us apart
After the chill and sweat of grit and guitars
The slow simmer of every mile you sat within reach

We talked over thick crusts in Pizza Huts
Over crooning, crying, rutting vocals oozing from Methuselah's speakers
Over its dented hubcaps, fenders built to elbow into parking spaces,
The hood where you lay smoking in the morning sun

"Such a Night"

First the rhythm of the horns, a bed of brass
a slink embedded in a thump, a slapped upright
humming rich and riotous, a growl

a voice vaults into the mix, baritone and kindling
the low-watt glow behind the grille of my desk radio

blinds blunt the streetlights, the traffic
the extinguished lamps amplify the hush
as the strings glide into their bend and the notes high up the neck
slide into the space between frets
where the shiver sleeps coiled

the current in my legs, the crossroads where they meet
where the music of moan locates its tonic
memories dormant in our skin arouse

how could an octave and a half house so much
pitch-perfect

Avishag the Shunamite
First Kings 1

I remember the king's soft palms
The long fingers that once plucked God's music from a harp
Muscled thighs that had straddled the thrones of queens

That legendary mast penetrating ports where veils fell on marble floors
    bringing the serpent to its feet
The sails now slumped at the base

When the sap ceased rising and the sun froze in the summer skies
I was found with my father's flocks in the fields
Wind rushing through the long grasses, olives greening under a broad
    blue noon

They placed me on a donkey's back with my father's kiss, with my
    sisters' tears, my mother's best dress riding behind me
Past the vineyards of clustered grapes that a young man's hands might
    cup
Slowly coaxing juice through the taut skins

Past the huts and yellowing hills, goats grazing and bucking
Carob pods hoarding honey, pomegranates stuffed stiff with seed

Ascending the sunflowered hills, hooves trampling the dust and earth,
    Jerusalem looming

Are my sisters home lugging buckets of milk from swollen udders,
    waiting for their bodies to bloom?

I remember the long walk to the royal chamber through the jasmine
    scented halls
Egyptian oils and rose water, cushions from Ethiopia
I soaked in the warm bath with these legs that had yet to grasp a man's
    waist as the goat thrust beneath me

Then we lay shepherd to shepherd, his soft stones out of their sling
And as my body blanketed his, the king inside the man quickened
I cradled his head, the once red curls now unfurling

That head that heard Goliath thud, his rippled bulk breaking his fall
That smelled the lion's breath panting towards his sheep halting its
    lunge in mid-leap
Those eyes that gaped at the glisten of Bathsheba's breasts rising from
    her rooftop bath
Breasts that would suckle kings

You and I

You are a potion of dark nail polish and dimmed lights
The slow dance of a dress falling round ankles
A Fauvist sunset lying on its back wearing only a crimson smile.

The groves are fig-heavy, the banks moist with the swelling current
I am the drunken river the ecstatic moment it dives off the cliff
You, the warm pool catching me softly.

Moses Took a Second Wife

Moses took a second wife
Under the shadow of the desert moon
His staff growing heavier each winter
When rains swim in brown rivers through the rough-cut mountains
And small plants plot their way out of the earth
While his people walked away from their past towards a greater past
And the sun walked quickly across the sky

Moses entered the tent of his second wife
Parting the darkened folds
And knew warmth
And knew earth like he hadn't since first shedding his shoes in a soft
    oasis of murmuring stalks
He remembered the buoyant Nile and
The moist limbs cradling his infant flesh

Moses opened his mouth and awe emerged
And his tongue, suddenly lightened,
Spoke secrets heard only at the birth of the ear
Moses filled his hands and felt his blood pool
He lifted his head in a laugh famed through the Fertile Crescent
And that laugh fathered all psalms
And that laugh was the rushing sound of the waters rivering Eden

Beard

My grandfather's beard smothered his chin, his cheeks, his eyes
    burning above his chiseled face
one photograph survives
cropped from a family portrait when the world feigned innocence
weeds wild on the sloped plains
collars buttoned closed with a tie

This is the man who lives on in my son's gaze
the laugh he allowed himself now amplified behind closed doors
a 14-year-old singing to himself
lyrics that sprint down the stairs, dance dizzy in a loose bathrobe

My grandfather's beard never scratched my flesh, never leaned down to
    bless me with a whisper
in an accent concocted from broken borders, forded rivers, the uprooted,
a continent at war with itself, the shudder of artillery

He bore the uniform of the Austro-Hungarian army
that would gut him the next war around
had the Germans not got there first –

hate is a zealous god

Your Small Hands

You began as a kiss in an English garden

The nurse held you up
Five ruddy pounds of instinct
And your one-syllable song
The father of all you will ever utter

You who gravitate towards the magnet of any open door
Dwarfing my dreams as you run, room to room, laughing over your
    shoulder,
Hoping to be chased

Your small lips coronate the breast
Your torso is an open embrace
Your hands lift your last Cheerios to my lips

A mirror is a baby babbling back at you
A piano, a singing oasis of wood and ivory
Every puddle a beach

You are a magician with nothing up your sleeve but
The softest skin

Red Walls

I hold your dancing hand in my father fingers
We are wearing sunset on our backs walking the boardwalk of many
    childhoods
By the hiss and hum of an indelible Atlantic
By the sand-drenched dunes

You are pulling me into tomorrow
In your hat of red mornings
And I am leap-happy in my dark jeans
Despite the splintered temples I coddle within me

In this jugular world of competing anthems
You carry a slew of cardinals under your hat
We paint your room with the tones of ripe apples
Gala upon gala

Praise

Praised be these orange walls, the sun peaking over the bedspread
Curtains catching the breeze in their diaphanous grip

Praised be the arch and heel, the translucent nails, the thighs' thrust,
    the ravenous motor where they meet
The grass rampant on hillsides, its soft urge

Praised be the diamond needle drawing music from the grooves of LPs,
    hoarding so much light in their shallow black channels
Praised be the voice's timbre, the solo song stark in the dark room
    but for the receiver's turquoise
Whispers floating face to face, the full-frontal embrace, the kiss
    and its slow release

Praised be the fallen fruit, the apricot's over-ripe pulp, its mulch-brown pit
The plum's peel of late summer sunset pierced, the tongue swimming
    in sweetness
Praised be the seeded furrows, gourds, roots, runners, vines plump with
    grapes
Light diving into the harbor, the stab of its shaft
The squall of seagulls, mussels free-falling in search of a rock on which
    to crack
A kayak's purple and shellac nosing up river

Praised be the pores' memories of high tide and coconut oil, plush
 towels pressed against ocean-chilled skin, the sweet diesel busload
 of kids climbing the pine-drenched hills
Praised be the congress of stars convening over Grand Canyon
The condor coasting on currents of air over the divine gash in the earth's gut

Praised be the horse's mane and muscle at full gallop, the body unbridled,
 the ballet leap, the moment when blood engorges
Praised be the first smile, gurgle, guffaw, handshake of strangers, tentative
 step from sea to solid earth, eyelids blinking at light

I crawled up the tiled roof to view the harbor, its narrow mouth,
 bungalows on its shores, masts, motors, moderate wakes under
 the unbroken blue
Praised be the voluminous sands, wind loosed on unruly lawns, acorns
 lodging an elaborate edifice in the jammed walls of their shells
Praised be the watermelon dawn, the hug of heat, the kiss of promiscuous
 rains

The God of Surprises

slipped loose at the shoveling
at the slow sliding
down cheeks
earth landing on the wooden casket

I gripped a shovel's neck
dropping its steel-cold handfuls
into the gaping ground
soil swallowing the past

the God of surprises woke me early
splashing me with sunlight
and an absence a father once filled
a voice I can't retrieve, advice I couldn't heed
a love too often camouflaged in conflict

those party photos peopled by the dead
where smiles and toasts "to life" called across a table
a hall filled with song, laughter, loud talk in Polish mixed with Yiddish

who would guess how they were orphaned,
what will propelled them to walk on
with hope buried alive all around them

they could not plaster over the fissures in the façade
undo the wars that forged them
the mass graves, the smoke and ash that is a birthright
I pass on second-hand

my son must sense something imported from Poland
beneath my Borough of Queens English
an undertone of exile
God stunned silent

Acknowledgements

I would like to thank the editors and staffs of the journals listed below in which the following poems were previously published, sometimes in slightly different versions.

Borders and Boundaries: "My Ex-Wedding"
The Jerusalem Review: "Avishag the Shunamite," "Blue Methuselah," "Headstone I," "Headstone II," "Pittsburgh," "Requiem for an Accent"
Muddy River Poetry Review: "Beard"
Mudfish: "My Mother's Song," "Résumé"
Newtown Literary: "Family Secrets," "My Father's Hands," "Red Hair," "Ode to Accents"
The Poeming Pigeon: "You and I"
Poetica: "The Belzer Rebbe Comes to Stryy," "The God of Surprises"
Referential Magazine: "I Am Therefore I Am"
Soul-Lit: "Moses Took a Second Wife"
Voices Israel: "Your Small Hands"

Further Acknowledgements

With a first book of poems coming at the age of 70, I've accumulated quite a number of people to whom I'm grateful. Rlene Dahlberg, a substitute teacher for one day in my tenth-grade English class in the spring of 1966 passed out a xeroxed copy of an e. e. cummings poem whose language thrilled me. That was my first true introduction to poetry. My older brother, Erwin, inspired me by his love of literature; he was one of the first people to whom I showed my writing regularly. Henry P. Wozniak, my outstanding English teacher the last three semesters in high school, was quite influential to me as an aspiring writer: he was not only someone to whom we could show our poems, but he took his students' love of writing seriously and was always generous and encouraging. He always made time for us.

The first day of my mandatory freshman "Introduction to Poetry" class, my professor handed out xeroxed copies of "A Supermarket in California" by Allen Ginsberg because we hadn't gotten textbooks yet and I fell in love with that poem. I was well-aware of Ginsberg as a prominent countercultural figure but had never read anything by him. Another professor, Gerry Meyers, with whom I never took a class, was kind enough to read and critique my work periodically.

During the summer of 1981, I had the good fortune of studying with Ginsberg at Naropa Institute in Boulder, Colorado. Given my car and his need for transportation, I was privileged to be Allen's occasional "driver" – our first trip being to a supermarket in Colorado! I will always be grateful for his candid weekly critiques of my writing which were enormously beneficial. A few years later, I studied at NYU with Yehuda Amichai and Philip Levine. Their wisdom and broad appreciation of poetry was inspirational. I am similarly thankful for having had the opportunity to study with Edward Hirsch at Breadloaf. Ed's talent, devotion, and deep knowledge of poetry have meant a great deal to me.

I am also grateful for the time and space to write afforded by residencies at the Millay Colony for the Arts, Blue Mountain Center, and the Arad Arts Project, experiences which were idyllic and transformational.

Much more recently, I was a student in the MFA Program for Writers at Warren Wilson College, which was everything I hoped for and more. I feel indebted to Ellen Bryant Voigt and Debra Allbery for an incredible program and especially to my wonderful supervisors at Warren Wilson: Brooks Haxton, Alan Williamson, Daisy Fried, and Alan Shapiro.
I want to express my deep appreciation to three people who supported me in my dreams of writing through many years: Ellen Waldman, Olga Cheselka, and Ernest Fried.

I am very grateful to the following poets whose feedback on my manuscript in various stages was invaluable: Molly Peacock, Nancy Pearson, and Helena Mesa.

I would like to thank my fellow travelers in the pursuit and love of poetry whose support and friendship make a big difference: Dan Alter, Rabbi Leila Gal Berner, Robin Rosen Chang, Nicole Chvatal, Ona Gritz, Jill Klein, Deborah Leipziger, Cecille Marcato, Trish Marshall, David Mills, Amanda Newell, Binnie Pasquier, Rabbi Jim Rosenberg, Susan Jo Russell, and Shannon K. Winston.

To all the wonderful, talented people at Passager Books who have made this book a reality: Mary Azrael, Christine Drawl, Rosanne Singer, Pantea Tofangchi, and especially Kendra Kopelke: You have made a lifelong dream come true. I can't thank you enough.

To my wife, Shoshana, and our son Lev – your daily love, support, and inspiration sustain me more than I can possibly express.

Top left to right: Elber with his mother, father and brother, Erwin, in 1958; Elber in 1972; 1983; and 1993.

photo by Shoshana Brown

Mark Elber was born and raised in Queens, New York City to Holocaust survivors and grew up hearing Polish, Yiddish, German, Russian, and English spoken at home. Rather than following his father's and brother's path into the medical profession, Mark pursued philosophy, Jewish mysticism, poetry, and music. He studied philosophy at the University of Pennsylvania, Kabbalah at Hebrew University in Jerusalem, and years later received his MFA from the Program for Writers at Warren Wilson College. In the intervening years, Mark was involved with forming two rock bands, songwriting, and becoming a rabbi. He is the author of *The Everything Kabbalah Book* and *The Sacred Now: Cultivating Jewish Spiritual Consciousness*. Mark lives with his wife, Shoshana Brown, and their son, Lev, in Fall River, MA, where Mark and Shoshana are the rabbi and cantor at Temple Beth El.

In legends, the crane stands for longevity, peace, harmony, good fortune and fidelity. A high flyer, it is cherished for its ability to see both heaven and earth. These ancient, magnificent birds, so crucial in the wild as an "umbrella species," are now endangered and must be protected.

Passager Books is dedicated to making public the passions of a generation vital to our survival.

If you would like to support Passager Books, please visit our website www.passagerbooks.com or email us at editors@passagerbooks.com.

Headstone was designed and typeset by Christine Drawl using Adobe InDesign. The pages are set in Adobe Garamond Pro and Optima.

The cover art is a 27" x 19" painting titled *All in a Day* by Margaret Singer (1921-2019). Born in Friedentstal, Germany, Singer escaped the Nazis in 1939 and eventually made her way to Santa Barbara, CA, where she became a poet, painter and teacher, inspired every day by the light streaming through windows. More about her life and work can be found at: https://jewishsantabarbara.org/margaret-singer

Printed in 2022 by Spencer Printing, Honesdale, PA.

Also From Passager

The Solitude of Memory
poems by MICHAEL MILLER

The Poets of Ingleside at Rock Creek
an anthology edited by CELIA CRAWFORD & MOLLY QUINN

Grandfather's Mandolin
poems by FRAN MARKOVER

Ox Horn Bend
memoir by ROY CHENG TSUNG

Tidal Wave
poems by DENNIS H. LEE

Prayers of Little Consequence
poems by GILBERT ARZOLA

Days of Blue and Flame
poems by SARAH YERKES

Taproot
poems by KATHY MANGAN

The Uncorrected Eye
poems by HARRY BAULD

Old Women Talking
poems by WILDERNESS SARCHILD

Prickly Roses: Stories from a Life
a memoir by JOYCE ABELL

A Sunday in Purgatory
poems by HENRY MORGENTHAU III

A Hinge of Joy, second edition
poems by JEAN L. CONNOR

The Three O'Clock Bird
poems by ANNE FRYDMAN

Finding Mr. Rightstein
a memoir by NANCY DAVIDOFF KELTON

Gathering the Soft
poems by BECKY DENNISON SAKELLARIOU
artwork by TANDY ZORBA

The Chugalug King & Other Stories
short stories by ANDREW BROWN

Little Miracles
poems by JAMES K. ZIMMERMAN

The Want Fire
poems by JENNIFER WALLACE

Never the Loss of Wings
poems by MARYHELEN SNYDER

Because There Is No Return
poems by DIANA ANHALT

Beyond Lowu Bridge
memoir by ROY CHENG TSUNG

Nightbook
poems by STEVE MATANLE

A Little Breast Music
poems by SHIRLEY J. BREWER

Perris, California
poems by NORMA CHAPMAN

Everything Is True at Once
poems by BART GALLE

Keeping Time: 150 Years of Journal Writing
edited by MARY AZRAEL & KENDRA KOPELKE

Burning Bright: Celebrating Older Voices
poems, fiction & memoir
edited by MARY AZRAEL & KENDRA KOPELKE

Hot Flash Sonnets
poems by MOIRA EGAN

Improvise in the Amen Corner
poems & drawings by LARNELL CUSTIS BUTLER

A Cartography of Peace
poems by JEAN L. CONNOR

Elber with his son, Lev, 2008. Photo by Shoshana Brown.

"You are pulling me into tomorrow
In your hat of red mornings"

from "Red Walls"